Alexander
HamiLToN

Alexander
HamiLTON

by James Buckley Jr.

Illustrated by Charlotte Ager

Senior Editor Shannon Beatty
Senior Designer Joanne Clark

Editor Abhijit Dutta
Senior Editors Marie Greenwood, Roohi Sehgal
Art Editor Kanika Kalra
Jacket Coordinator Issy Walsh
Jacket Designer Dheeraj Arora
DTP Designers Mrinmoy Mazumdar, Sachin Gupta
Picture Researcher Aditya Katyal
Pre-Producer Sophie Chatellier
Producer Basia Ossowska
Managing Editors Laura Gilbert, Monica Saigal
Deputy Managing Art Editor Ivy Sengupta
Managing Art Editor Diane Peyton Jones
Delhi Team Head Malavika Talukder
Creative Director Helen Senior
Publishing Director Sarah Larter

Subject Consultant Nicole Scholet de Villavicencio
Literacy Consultant Stephanie Laird

First American Edition, 2019
Published in the United States by DK Publishing
1450 Broadway, New York, New York 10018

Copyright © 2019 Dorling Kindersley Limited
DK, a Division of Penguin Random House LLC
19 20 21 22 23 10 9 8 7 6 5 4 3 2 1
001–311578–Apr/2019

A catalog record for this book is available from the Library of Congress.
ISBN: 978-1-4654-7961-7 (Paperback)
ISBN: 978-1-4654-7960-0 (Hardcover)

DK books are available at special discounts when purchased in bulk for sales promotions,
premiums, fund-raising, or educational use. For details, contact:
DK Publishing Special Markets,
345 Hudson Street, New York, New York 10014
SpecialSales@dk.com

Printed and bound in China

A WORLD OF IDEAS:
SEE ALL THERE IS TO KNOW

www.dk.com

Dear Reader,

You're probably reading this because you've heard of the Broadway musical about Alexander Hamilton. But his story is much more than snappy lyrics and people dancing in wigs and ball gowns. From his birth on a Caribbean island to his death in a duel in New Jersey, Alexander believed that he had a special role to play in history. He was determined to make a mark on the world, and in the American Revolution and its aftermath, he found a way. Intelligent, well-read, determined, and stubborn, he used his power with words to help create a country that continues to work pretty much like he said it should.

In this story, you can relive the beginning of the American Revolution, find out Alexander's place in it, and discover that his greatest love was his honor. Alexander was a complicated, intense person who lived one of the most remarkable lives in American history— one that's really worth singing about.

James Buckley Jr.

The life of... Alexander **Hamilton**

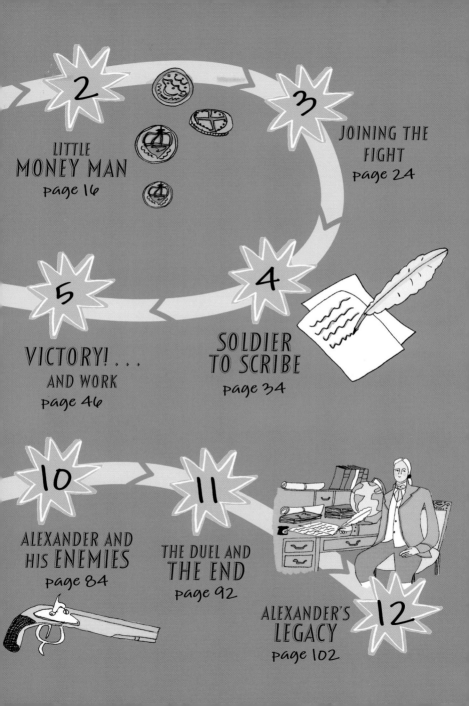

1

A bumpy start

Alexander Hamilton had a tough start to an amazing life. He lost his parents as a boy, but he overcame tragedy to do great things.

In about 1750, a man from Scotland set out to make his fortune in the New World, which is what Europeans named the Americas and the islands around them. James Hamilton left his home in chilly Scotland for the warm and balmy island of Nevis in the Caribbean Sea. He was not alone—thousands of people from Great Britain and other countries in Europe had traveled across the Atlantic Ocean in the previous century. The New World was brimming with opportunity, from Canada in the north, through the English-owned lands that would form the United States, to the islands dotting the southern sea.

On Nevis, James met a woman whose parents had been among those who had come across earlier. The woman's name was Rachael Faucette, and her mother was English and her father was French. She had been married, but in a rare thing for this time, she and her husband had gotten a divorce. According to the laws of the colony, being divorced meant that she could not get married again. However, she fell in love with James and they became a couple—and then they became parents.

Having children without being married was frowned upon back in those days. Children born of such unions were called "illegitimate."

what is a colony?

Any land or territory owned and controlled by another country. Nevis, where Alexander's parents lived, was a British colony.

9

These kids started life at a disadvantage because they were in a lower social position than their peers. In other words, people looked down on anyone who was illegitimate.

James and Rachael had two sons— one was named James, and the other was Alexander. The hero of our story, Alexander, was the younger of the two boys, and he was born on January 11 on Nevis—he said he was

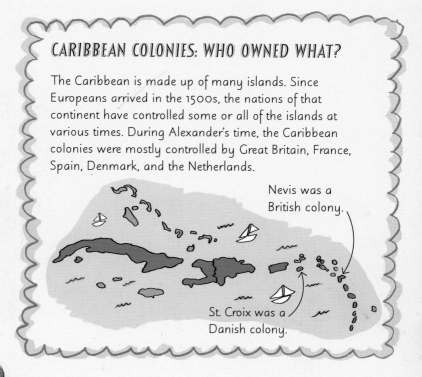

CARIBBEAN COLONIES: WHO OWNED WHAT?

The Caribbean is made up of many islands. Since Europeans arrived in the 1500s, the nations of that continent have controlled some or all of the islands at various times. During Alexander's time, the Caribbean colonies were mostly controlled by Great Britain, France, Spain, Denmark, and the Netherlands.

Nevis was a British colony.

St. Croix was a Danish colony.

The island of Nevis, where Alexander was born, was a British colony at the time.

born in 1757, though one record suggested it was 1755. The Hamilton family moved to a nearby island, St. Croix, when Alexander's father James got a new business opportunity. Unfortunately, not long after they moved, James abandoned his family and moved to another nearby island in 1766. Rachael and her two young sons were left all alone, and in a terrible situation. As social outcasts, the boys were not even allowed to go to the local Christian school. Then things got even worse.

Rachael's ex-husband, Peter Lavien, made a claim on what little money she had, which left her penniless. Rachael opened a shop to try to make money to care for her children. She had inherited several slaves from her family, and they worked with her in the house and shop.

SLAVERY

Slavery is when a person is controlled and "owned" by another. This horrendous practice violates people's basic human rights. Starting in the 1500s, Europeans sailed in ships to Africa, captured people there, and made them into slaves in the New World colonies. Over more than 300 years, more than 12 million people were enslaved. Slavery didn't officially end in the United States until 1865!

The Caribbean islands were often the first stop for the slave ships after they left Africa.

DID YOU KNOW?

In 1756, around the time Alexander was born, more than 13,000 slaves lived in New York City.

In nearly every colony in the New World, black Africans were bought and sold and forced to work on plantations, which were big farms. In towns and cities, slaves were forced to work in shops, like the one owned by the Hamiltons. It was a cruel and awful business. Young Alexander, in fact, despised it from the start.

The Hamiltons' shop struggled, and then things got really bad. Less than a year after James left her, Rachael died of a fever. Alexander himself got very sick, too, but being younger, he was stronger and he eventually recovered. Alexander's brother, James, did not get sick, but he had to watch it all in horror.

The boys were taken in by a cousin, but shortly after that, he took his own life. Within the span of about 18 months, Alexander and James went from being intelligent, active young boys with a mother and father in a nice house, to poor, unloved orphans. Luckily for Alexander, he was still intelligent and active.

Though he and his brother had been educated at home, Alexander had learned a lot from his schooling, including how to speak French from his mother. Young Alexander was a voracious reader, flying through books on history, politics, language, and more. His intelligence, love of words and ideas, and his strong belief in himself would be his tickets out of his tough situation.

Little money man

Who knew a hurricane could be a good thing? A natural disaster and Alexander's bright mind set him on a new and hopeful path.

After his father abandoned them, and then the deaths of his mother and cousin, Alexander and his brother were truly alone. They needed a new place to live. He and his brother had no other relatives who could take them in.

Luckily for them, a merchant named Thomas Stevens had known their mother, Rachael. Thomas heard about their plight, and he brought both boys to live with his family.

That family included a boy only a couple of years older than Alexander. His name was Edward "Neddy" Stevens, and he became Alexander's best friend. The pair wandered the island together, ate with the Stevens family, and talked about their plans.

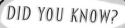

Thomas arranged to have James made an apprentice to a carpenter. An apprentice is a trainee who learns a trade by helping a skilled craftsperson on the job. Alexander had already been working before his mother died—with a merchant named Nicholas Cruger.

Cruger had moved from New York City to the Caribbean islands. With Cruger, Alexander quickly put his learning to work.

Nicholas Cruger

He was great with numbers, a key part of any business, and Cruger gave his young worker more and more responsibility.

One thing Alexander particularly enjoyed was working with the many types of money that flowed through the Cruger business. His business sold goods to and from other colonies, and each of those colonies used different types of money, from British pounds to French francs to Spanish pieces-of-eight.

HOW MUCH IS THAT?

Then and now, different countries had different kinds of coins and money. A coin from one country might equal six coins from another country. How different currencies relate to one another is the exchange rate.

British penny

French écu

Spanish colonial coin

Dutch guilder

Understanding how to compare the values of different currencies—the exchange rates— proved to be one of Alexander's special talents. This knowledge would come in handy later in his work with the American Treasury.

Cruger was lucky to have Alexander around, because in 1771, the merchant became very sick and had to return to his home in the English colony of New York to recover. He left the teenage Alexander in charge of his business.

Alexander took to the work with great energy, a trait he would show in all his life's endeavors. He managed the company accounts, sold the goods, and arranged ships and transport across the Atlantic Ocean and around the Caribbean. He, unfortunately, also

had to buy and sell slaves for Cruger, and he hated this part of the job. His experiences with slavery would later play a big part in his desire for freedom for the British colonists, white and black.

Through his work experience with Cruger, Alexander learned that there was a lot more to the world than just Nevis and St. Croix. His best friend, Edward Stevens, had already left the islands for the American colonies, and Alexander longed to join him. He had a growing sense of purpose and a desire to be noticed. These personality traits would become his trademark—for good and for bad—in his later life in America. First, however, he had to get there.

The islands of the Caribbean lie in the path of fierce storms called hurricanes. They swirl with high winds and kick up floods and surges of seawater. These storms are part of life in the islands. With one of the storms, however, the island's bad luck became good luck for Alexander.

On August 31, 1772, a terrible hurricane struck the region. High winds, heavy rain, and sweeping tides caused wreckage and death on a wide scale. Alexander and his brother were spared, but they knew many others whose lives had been destroyed.

Alexander was still writing to his father, James. He had apparently forgiven James. Alexander crafted a letter describing the hurricane and its aftermath, but before sending it, he showed it to

a local minister. The minister was so impressed with Alexander's writing skills that he said the letter should be published in the newspaper.

When islanders read the letter, they were astonished that the orphaned young man had such a wondrous talent. Several people, including a cousin of his named Ann, as well as Cruger, felt that they should do something to help Alexander get ahead in life. They gathered enough money to send him away to a university in the American colonies. This was Alexander's opportunity to show the world what he could do.

Joining the fight

Alexander arrived in New York in October 1772. He was determined to make a name for himself and to rise above his humble origins.

Alexander had connections in New Jersey, so he began his schooling there. He needed to catch up to other young men of the time, and prepare to apply to one of the top universities. He was a young man in a hurry. After several months of study, he tried to get into Princeton University, requesting that he move "from Class to Class with as much rapidity as his exertions would enable him to do so." Princeton did not agree, and turned him down.

He tried to get into college again, this time by applying to

New York City's King's College, and was accepted. There he joined his old friend from St. Croix, Edward Stevens. Alexander also made friends with an outgoing Irishman named Hercules Mulligan. Together, the young men found themselves at the center of a world of change.

In the early 1770s, as Alexander was seeing his own life change so radically, the colonists in America were starting to talk about radical change of their own. At the time, the American colonies were owned by Great Britain. The British made a series of unpopular decisions, mostly about imposing

King's College would later be called Columbia University.

new taxes, or fees, on the American colonists. Because of this, many Americans wanted freedom from Great Britain. New York was one place where a lot of this "revolutionary" talk happened. Hercules was part of a group called the Sons of Liberty, and a similar group in Boston pulled off the Boston Tea Party.

From his time on the islands, Alexander knew that freedom was worth fighting for.

BOSTON TEA PARTY

The British made money by putting taxes on the tea that the colonists loved. In protest, a group of colonists—disguised as Native Americans for some reason—climbed onto British ships in the harbor and tossed bales of tea into the water.

The Boston Tea Party took place on December 16, 1773.

He soon found that his way with words gave him the ability to express his opinions on why freedom was so important.

In the city, there were outdoor stages where anyone could step up and give his point of view. Listeners were amazed that this "collegian" was such a wonderful, eloquent speaker, and that he was so forward-thinking in his ideas. Alexander also wrote letters and articles calling for a change in government. He believed that the slaves he had seen back on Nevis and St. Croix had a lot in common with the colonists living under the rule of Great Britain. "Are you willing to become slaves?" he wrote. "Will you give up? Americans are entitled to freedom!" He signed his letters "A Friend of America."

what is a collegian? Someone who attends college or university. As a student, Alexander was a collegian.

Alexander and the young men did more than just talk and write about freedom. They wanted to take action. So they formed a group they called the Hearts of Oak to practice being soldiers for a war they felt was coming soon.

In April 1775, war did indeed come. The colonists were angry about the high taxes they had to pay Great Britain, and this led to conflict. On April 19, 1775, the Revolutionary War (1775–83) started with the "shot heard round the world" in a clash between the American and British forces at Lexington and Concord in Massachusetts.

The first shots on the Lexington battlefield were fired early in the morning on April 19, 1775.

"I would die to preserve the law upon a solid foundation; but take away liberty, and the foundation is destroyed."

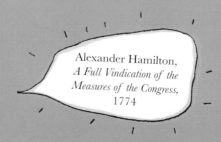

Alexander Hamilton,
*A Full Vindication of the
Measures of the Congress,*
1774

To fight the war, the Continental Congress, which included representatives from the 13 British colonies, formed the Continental Army. This new army would be tasked with fighting the British, and they would be led by a man named George Washington.

In New York City, the Hearts of Oak waited for a chance to play their part in the war. In August, led by Alexander and Hercules, they pulled off a raid, sneaking into a warehouse to steal 10 cannons from the British to give to the American forces. In March 1776, Alexander left college to join the Continental Army. His intelligence, time with the Oaks, and skill with numbers earned him a spot as a captain in the artillery, the part of the army that fired cannons.

HEARTS OF OAK

The name "hearts of oak" has a long history. British sailors were nicknamed "hearts of oak" after the strongest type of wood used to make ships. It was also the name of a song often heard on British Navy ships. Having a heart of oak meant that you were strong, brave, and true.

During the Revolutionary War, Alexander was a captain in the artillery.

31

On July 9, 1776, Alexander was among the assembled American troops who stood at attention with their leader, General George Washington. The men were gathered to hear the Declaration of Independence read aloud for the first time in New York City. It had been passed by the Continental Congress on July 4. The important and memorable words of that declaration rang out on the King's College commons (a central gathering place), and from there, around the world.

DECLARATION OF INDEPENDENCE

This was one of the most important documents in modern world history. Written by Thomas Jefferson for the Continental Congress, it said that the American colonies were no longer owned by Great Britain.

Back when Alexander had been living on St. Croix, he had written to his friend Edward. In the letter, Alexander yearned for something that would bring him out of the islands and give him a chance to distinguish himself. "I wish there was a war," he wrote.

Thanks in part to the words written in the Declaration of Independence, Alexander's wish had finally come true.

Soldier to **scribe**

The war years kept Alexander very busy, on and off the battlefield. This time also established the two most important relationships of his life.

The war did not start out well for the Americans, who were led by George Washington. He was based in New York City, so the British made it their mission to drive him out of there. After taking control of Boston following the Battle of Bunker Hill in 1775, the British troops moved south toward Manhattan.

BATTLE OF BUNKER HILL

When is a loss a win? When you do so well, you set yourself up to win later. The British won the Battle of Bunker Hill. The Americans did so well, however, that they got the courage to fight again.

The small Continental Army around General Washington, including Alexander and his cannons, was no match for the mighty British.

British troops first chased the American soldiers off Long Island, to the east of New York City. Then they crossed the East River onto the island of Manhattan itself, marching south toward the tip of the island, pushing aside all resistance. By the fall of 1776, the Continental Army, including Washington and Alexander, was fleeing south through New Jersey.

what is a general? A military term for a high-ranking army officer who plans attacks and leads troops. Alexander reported to General Washington.

Washington knew that he needed to find a way to fight back. Winter was coming and with it bad weather that would make fighting even harder. He came up with a plan and would need Alexander's help.

Washington learned that a large troop of Hessian soldiers would be near Trenton, New Jersey, for Christmas. The general came up with a plan to sneak up on the enemy at night

WHO WERE HESSIANS?

Soldiers who will fight for any country that pays them are called mercenaries. They have been part of war for centuries. In the Revolutionary War, the British hired Germans called Hessians to fight against the colonists. They were only partly mercenaries, however. The soldiers' wages were actually paid by the German princes— but the British paid the princes much more!

by crossing the icy Delaware River across from the camp. What was Alexander's role in all this? Once the fighting started, he was to direct his cannon fire to prevent reinforcements from joining on the British side.

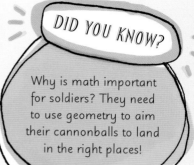

DID YOU KNOW?

Why is math important for soldiers? They need to use geometry to aim their cannonballs to land in the right places!

There is a famous painting of this historic scene (see pages 38–39). The painting, by Emanuel Leutze, was not 100 percent accurate, but it did symbolize the passionate and determined attitude of the American soldiers. (Also, Washington didn't stand up in the boat, that type of flag didn't exist in 1776, and the men used a lot more than just five oars!) Climbing into rickety wooden boats, some of which were carrying unsteady horses or massive cannons, and crossing a freezing-cold river in the dark? That took guts.

what are reinforcements?

When armies are running short of soldiers, they call for more to join them. These added troops are called reinforcements.

Washington Crossing the Delaware (1851) is a well-known painting by German–American painter Emanuel Leutze. It is an idealized, or glamorized, picture of the Americans on their way to battle the Hessians at Trenton, New Jersey.

The surprise attack was a complete success. Washington's army followed it with another attack, this time on the nearby town of Princeton. In fact, Princeton University, the school that had rejected Alexander, was housing British troops. After the battles, Alexander was made a lieutenant colonel—a big promotion for someone so young (he was 20 or 22, depending on when he was actually born).

Following the successful battles in New Jersey, Washington had a special job for his new colonel. It was not one that Alexander actually wanted. He felt that his path to fame and success was on the battlefield. Back on St. Croix, Alexander had read about ancient Roman generals and famous military leaders.

Washington, however, wanted Alexander not for his bravery, but for his impressive brain. He appointed the excellent young writer and thinker as his personal assistant, called an aide-de-camp, in the army.

For the next four or so years, Alexander was nearly always at Washington's side. He wrote many of Washington's letters, and he also took down his orders for the troops. He helped to arrange the many things that an army on the move needs to survive. Alexander made sure the troops had enough food, clothing, and ammunition. He also bought whatever else the army needed from merchants.

American military leader and first president, George Washington was an important person in Alexander's life.

Many writers have looked at Washington as the father that Alexander never really had. Washington was more than 20 years older than Alexander, and the general had already served in the French and Indian War (1754–63). He knew how to gather men around him and to lead them. In fact, Washington did refer to the men closest to him in the army as his "family." (The great general and later first president had no children of his own.) Alexander did look up to Washington, and he served him well and with vigor. However, more than anyone else around him, Alexander was his own man, convinced of his intelligence and sure that he knew best. He pushed those feelings aside to serve the cause of liberty he believed in, but he always wished to be back on the battlefield.

In 1779, while on his travels with Washington, Alexander met a young woman named Elizabeth (Eliza) Schuyler. He had

Elizabeth (Eliza) Schuyler

been first introduced to her in 1777, but two years later he still remembered her. When stationed near her house in the winter, he visited and wrote to her often. For Alexander to woo her was a stretch, however. At the time, it was considered important for people to marry within their own social class. Men were not supposed to marry for love, but for the right connection. His birth outside the American colonies to unmarried parents counted against him in social circles, though not in the army. Still, the couple overcame these various prejudices and were married in 1780.

"Elizabeth is most unmercifully handsome . . . with good nature, affability, and vivacity."

Alexander Hamilton, in a letter to Elizabeth's sister, Margarita

Victory! . . . and work

This was a very busy time for Alexander. After he served in the war, he became a parent and a lawyer, and he helped to found a new country!

The war turned for the American side as the 1770s ended, and by 1781 it looked like they might actually have a chance at winning. As important as he had been to the war effort in his role as an aide-de-camp and clerk, Alexander wanted another chance at glory. He wanted to lead and fight on the battlefield.

In early 1781, Alexander found an excuse to resign from Washington's staff. Washington did not want to lose his valuable friend, so he appointed Alexander to lead a battalion.

What is a battalion?

Armies are divided up into groups of soldiers. When several small groups are combined, they form a larger group called a battalion.

Alexander and Washington would fight together in a battle at Yorktown, Virginia. At the Battle of Yorktown, the Americans had trapped the British on a peninsula (a strip of land jutting into the water) on the Atlantic coast. With help from the French Navy, the Americans hoped this would be the final battle of the war.

DID YOU KNOW?

The French joined the Americans in the fight against the British in 1778.

During the Battle of Yorktown in Virginia, Alexander had a chance to lead his troops into battle against the British Army.

Alexander's forces were sent to attack a redoubt, a large fortress that protected soldiers. Though he had been carrying little more than a pen for years, Alexander snatched up his sword and led his men into battle as they stormed over the dirt. They swarmed over the British soldiers and captured their enemies.

This important part of the battle basically won the war for the Americans. Stuck on the peninsula, the British troops tried to escape by sea. As the Americans attacked by land, French ships prevented British ships from sailing to the rescue. Trapped between the Americans and the French, the British had to surrender.

Alexander wrote to his wife, Eliza, that she could read all about the victory in the newspaper (more fame!), but he promised her that "there will be, I assure you, nothing more of this kind."

Instead, Alexander would become part of a less violent, but equally important, struggle. He had been a part of the revolution from the very beginning, and he was there on the battlefield when it ended. In the years ahead, he would put his talents to work, making sure that all the death, hardship, and struggle during the war was really worth it.

The Americans had defeated the British Army, it was true. However, they still had a lot of work to do. No country had ever thrown off British rule. There was no plan for what to do next—how to set up a government, make laws, and protect the new nation.

"Vigor of government is essential to the security of liberty."

Alexander Hamilton,
Federalist No. 1,
"General Introduction,"
1787

Alexander returned to New York City with Eliza and their son Philip (born in 1782). His next plan was to become a lawyer. He was in a hurry to do so, just as he had been with his earlier education. His military service counted toward the requirements to become a lawyer, which meant he got his license to practice law quickly.

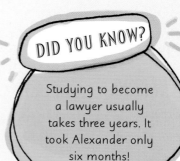

DID YOU KNOW?

Studying to become a lawyer usually takes three years. It took Alexander only six months!

He set about earning money to support his family, taking a variety of cases. A few of his clients were controversial. Tories were colonists who had remained loyal to England during the Revolutionary War. After the war was over, some local lawmakers tried to take money and goods from the Tories. Alexander defended some of them against these actions in court. So why was this controversial? Tories were seen as enemies, and Alexander was

what does controversial mean?

Something that causes disagreement. Some of Alexander's legal cases were controversial.

taking their side. To Alexander, however, he was taking the side of doing the right thing. He didn't think that taking money from his fellow Americans was right.

He also had time to turn his attention back to a cause he had first learned about, and despised, as a boy—slavery. In 1785, Alexander and others founded the first antislavery organization in New York City—the New York Manumission Society. They raised awareness about the horrible nature of slavery and tried to pass laws banning it, or making it illegal, in New York.

Alexander was also brought in to write the constitution (a document that lays out basic,

NEW YORK MANUMISSION SOCIETY

This group worked to protect people of African descent living in New York City. Astonishingly, some of the Manumission Society founders owned slaves themselves! Alexander tried to pass a rule that they had to release them but it was voted down. In 1799, a law was passed that gradually outlawed slavery in New York State.

Alexander reading from the new constitution of the
Bank of New York, which he'd written.

founding rules), of the new Bank of New York,
a company that still exists today. He drew on
the lessons he had learned in the merchant's
offices on St. Croix, and on the studying he had
done in the years since. Also, during the war,
he had seen the importance of money to a
country—Washington's army often suffered
from a lack of funds for vital food, gear, and
transportation. Alexander believed strongly that
the new American nation had to have a strong

financial structure if it was to succeed.
A bank like this one was a first step.

As Alexander worked to set up his new life in
New York, people around the nation were talking
about how to strengthen America's new status
as a free country. Not surprisingly, Alexander
had many opinions on the matter. His skill
with words, experience, and intelligence
led him to be named a New York State
representative to the Constitutional
Convention in 1787. This important
meeting was held in Philadelphia to form a
new national government. The members
of the Constitutional Convention would
later be known as the Founding Fathers of
the United States.

Though he was representing New York
State, Alexander's status as a person born
outside the colonies helped him in the early
days. This was because he was not linked
by loyalty to a single state, as the other
Founding Fathers were. For example, Benjamin
Franklin was connected to Pennsylvania, and

Washington and Thomas Jefferson were linked to Virginia. Alexander saw that the best way forward was for everyone to retrain themselves to have a single loyalty to the United States, and not to their individual states. Alexander supported a strong central government, and at the convention, he got a chance to carry his ideas forward.

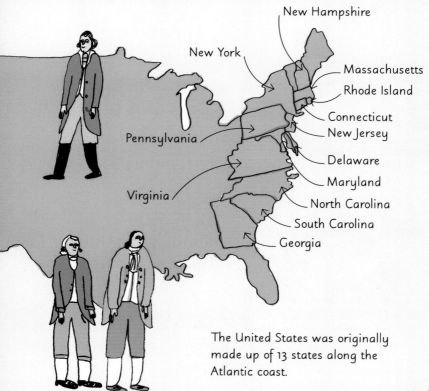

New Hampshire

New York

Massachusetts

Rhode Island

Connecticut

New Jersey

Pennsylvania

Delaware

Maryland

Virginia

North Carolina

South Carolina

Georgia

The United States was originally made up of 13 states along the Atlantic coast.

Chapter

Makin' the laws

In Philadelphia in May 1787, 55 men gathered together to create a constitution, or a group of laws that would govern the new United States.

It was a tough job. Every state had its own needs and wants. They wanted to make sure that they got to do what they wanted, but they also knew that they had to make rules to work together. It was the "United" States, after all, so they would have to find a way to agree on things.

The men divided into two major groups. One wanted the states to be more powerful individually than the national government— they were the states' rights or Anti-Federalist group. The other group wanted a very strong national, or federal, government. They were called the Federalists, and Alexander was one of the leaders of this group.

56

They finally came to a compromise. Delegates, or representatives, including James Madison, made a plan for a three-part government—the president (executive branch), the courts (judicial branch), and the legislature (legislative branch), who would make the laws. The legislative branch was then divided into two—the House of Representatives, where a state's population determines how many votes it gets, and the Senate, with two votes per state.

CHECKS AND BALANCES

The Founding Fathers didn't want any single part of the government to have all the power. So the three parts are meant to oversee one another so no branch gets too strong. This idea is known as "checks and balances."

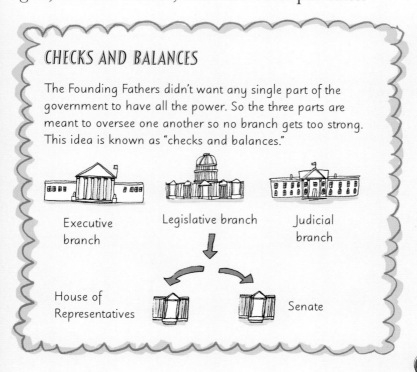

Executive branch

Legislative branch

Judicial branch

House of Representatives

Senate

The aim was to make sure that big states with a lot of people did not make all the laws thanks to their large size. The Senate gave every state, of any size, equal representation.

The Federalists, however, got much of what they wanted. The Constitution that was passed included rules that gave the federal government a lot of power, especially over war, money, trade, and international relations.

The United States Capitol Building in Washington, D.C., is where the Senate and House of Representatives meet.

Washington and others at the Constitutional Convention.

Once the Constitution was passed, or approved, by the Constitutional Convention, it had to be ratified by the states. "Ratified" means that each state got to vote on whether to accept or reject the Constitution. Over the next year or so, the debates raged up and down the coast. Alexander and the other delegates had to convince at least nine of the 13 states to vote for the Constitution. Without those votes in their favor, all the work they had done would be for nothing.

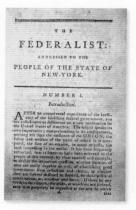

Alexander aimed to influence voters with the *Federalist Papers*.

To help voters decide, Alexander led a small group in writing what came to be called the *Federalist Papers*. These were a series of articles that asked and answered questions about how the new Constitution would work, how states would work together, and how the federal government would operate.

Oddly, most Americans did not read or even hear about the *Federalist Papers*. The articles had a big impact in New York City, where they were published widely, and among the leaders of the nation. However, they were published in only a few newspapers in big cities. In fact, for most of the next 150 to 200 years, the *Federalist Papers* were not really used that much. However, in recent decades, people called "originalists" have looked back at them to make sure today's America is exactly what the Founding Fathers wanted. They have examined the 85 different *Federalist Papers* for evidence and arguments on various issues.

In upstate New York, people were mostly against the Constitution, but New York City's residents strongly supported it. Alexander himself was chosen to lead New York City's delegation at the state gathering that would vote on ratification, or formal approval.

Alexander's persuasion worked. New York State voted in favor of the Constitution. He was celebrated in New York City for his work with a parade that included a giant model ship being towed through the streets. "HAMILTON" was written on the sides. (Some people even wanted to rename New York as "Hamiltonia." Obviously, they did not get their way.)

"... [W]e have fought side by side to make America free, let us hand in hand struggle to make her happy."

Alexander Hamilton, in a letter to John Laurens, 1782

On June 21, 1788, New Hampshire became the last needed state to ratify the Constitution. With this ninth state's approval, the Constitution became the law of the land and founding document of the United States. After the first national election, on April 30, 1789, George Washington was sworn in as the first president of the United States. One of the first people Washington called on for help was his old aide-de-camp—Alexander.

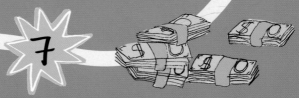

Big money man

President Washington had big plans for his trusted wartime assistant. He put Alexander in charge of America's money.

President Washington appointed Alexander to be the first Secretary of the Treasury—the office that is responsible for America's money. What Alexander quickly discovered, however, was that America did not have a lot of it.

Following the successful war, the new nation owed debts to many other countries from whom it had borrowed money to fight the British. The individual states and the federal government, in the form of the Continental Congress during the war, all owed more money than they had.

The federal government also owed a lot of money to the people who had fought in the war, some of whom went years without pay.

James Madison

Once again, the two different American political groups disagreed about what to do. Led by Madison, the Anti-Federalists did not want the new national government to deal with all this debt. Alexander and the Federalists, however, wanted to take it all on, including the money owed by the states.

His plan was known as "assumption," which means to take on something that is not yours. It was a bold idea and he backed it up with a plan to sell bonds (or IOUs) that would pay back all the national debt over time. At first, Alexander's plan did not make it past Congress. He saw an opportunity, however, to make a deal.

What is Congress?

The collective name for the two parts of the United States' legislature—the Senate and the House of Representatives.

He was afraid that without dealing with its money problems, the new nation would not succeed. Alexander also knew that Madison and Thomas Jefferson, the Secretary of State (in charge of relationships and deals with other countries), wanted something. Both men were from Virginia and they wanted the nation's capital to be located in, or at least near, their home state. In 1789, the United States' first capital was New York City (and from 1790–1800, the capital was Philadelphia).

Alexander arranged a meeting at which he agreed to get the capital moved in return for Madison and his allies backing Alexander's plan to take on the national debt. The new capital would be named for Washington, but also called D.C., for District of Columbia. That second name was for Christopher Columbus— back then still seen as the first European to "find" America.

Christopher Columbus

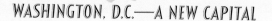

WASHINGTON, D.C.—A NEW CAPITAL

At their "dinner party meeting," Alexander, Madison, and Jefferson set up the new nation's capital, called the District of Columbia. It took land from Virginia and Maryland, so it was not part of any one state, but its own place. In the coming years, new buildings arose—the Capitol, the White House, the Supreme Court—and Washington, D.C., became a major center of political power.

The White House

The meeting, held one evening at Jefferson's house, made Alexander one of the most important people of the time. After taking on the national debt, Alexander's next big plan was to create a national bank to deal with the debt—the Bank of the United States.

The Federal Reserve
Bank has its
headquarters in
Washington, D.C.

FEDERAL RESERVE

1936

Today, Alexander's national bank is the basis for the Federal Reserve Bank—the most powerful financial institution in the country, if not the world. Without the deal, the power of the federal government to manage money in the new nation might have been lost. Alexander's experience back on St. Croix, working with money at Cruger's, came in handy. He knew that control of the flow of cash was essential.

Throughout it all, Washington's support proved vital to Alexander and his ideas. The general turned president trusted Alexander from their time together in the war. Over the next few years, Alexander was a key part of just about every decision President Washington made. Alexander's work was not finished, however, and he had other big ideas.

8

A mistake

In the 1780s, Alexander's work and home life bloomed. He and Eliza were building their family, but things were about to get complicated.

Alexander and Eliza had their first child, Philip, in 1782. By 1791, the couple had welcomed another three children into the world. (The Hamiltons would eventually have eight children, but at this point, they had four.) The family now lived in Philadelphia, Pennsylvania, which was the temporary national capital while Washington, D.C., was being built.

In the summer of 1791, the Hamilton family made a temporary change to their living arrangements. Eliza would escape the heat of the city by taking the kids away to

her parents' house in the countryside. Alexander
would stay behind in Philadelphia to work.

While there, a woman named Maria
Reynolds came to see Alexander. She asked
him for financial help, saying her husband
had left her. Alexander gave her money, and
the two became close. For a year, they had a
romance together, and he continued to give
her funds until he realized she was just interested
in the money. He ended the relationship, but it
would come back later to haunt him.

"I paid a high price for my folly," he said later. The true cost would not be known for years.

Back on the job, Alexander continued to press for new parts of the federal government to be created. Before the Constitution had passed, just about every state printed and minted, or manufactured, its own money. Alexander recognized the need for national United States money and helped form the first mint.

The first United States Mint was located in Philadelphia, Pennsylvania. This painting shows what the mint looked like in the late 1790s.

The United States government began minting its own national coins in 1792. Other countries' coins were still used—as long as they were made of gold or silver. From 1792 onward, though, United States' coins were considered the country's standard currency.

Another way the federal government controlled money was to charge a tax or duty (also called "customs") on goods that were brought into the country. People who owned shipping companies tried to avoid paying that tax by sneaking their ships into harbors.

To catch them, Alexander helped create a service of guard boats that could chase down ships trying to skip out on the taxes. Alexander also protected these ships by arranging to have new lighthouses built on key places along the Atlantic coastline. Today, those guard boats and lighthouses are part of the United States Coast Guard, or the USCG for short.

Alexander had new lighthouses built along the United States' shoreline. Light beams from lighthouses, such as this one at Cape Hatteras in North Carolina, help to guide and protect ships in dark or stormy conditions.

Chapter **9**

Tough times

The decade ahead would prove to be a difficult time for Alexander. He would face troubles in both his work and his personal life.

Alexander kept pushing to have the federal government do more and more. In 1791, he tried to get Congress to raise money to help develop new industries and manufacturers. It was a forward-thinking plan because, at the time, most people in America made their living by farming, not by making things.

His plan did not pass, which means it didn't get approved by Congress. However, it was a good example of the kind of big project that he wanted his new nation to take on.

Meanwhile, the split between Federalists, who were in charge of the national government, and Anti-Federalists widened. Madison and Jefferson organized the Anti-Federalists into the Democratic Republican Party. (They were different from today's Democrats and Republicans.) Alexander still helped lead the Federalists.

Among the Democratic Republicans was a New York politician named Aaron Burr. Alexander did not trust Burr one bit. The feeling was mutual. Burr had beaten Alexander's father-in-law, Philip Schuyler, in an election in 1789. At the time, Alexander wrote about Burr, "He is for or against nothing,

Aaron Burr

but as it suits his interest or ambition . . . I feel it is a religious duty to oppose his career." (These strong feelings about Burr would come up again later in Alexander's life, and this time with terrible consequences.)

The political fighting, and tiredness brought on by long years of work, led Alexander to resign from the Treasury in 1795. He wanted to spend more time with his wife and children.

However, Alexander's past actions got him into trouble. In 1797, letters he had written to the woman with whom he'd had a relationship, Maria Reynolds, were made public. His opponents accused him of stealing government money to pay her off. In response, Alexander did a surprising thing—he wrote a booklet in which

he admitted having an affair with her. However, he denied that any of the money came from the government. He said that the only money he paid was from himself.

It was shocking to make such an admission. Alexander even published *more* letters that Maria sent to him, and some of them were quite embarrassing for him. He appeared to be more concerned with his honor in government and finance than with his honor in marriage.

In the end, though, his reputation was seriously hurt. Alexander had overcome the prejudice of being both illegitimate and an immigrant only to find himself scorned for cheating on his wife.

Alexander's wife, Eliza, remained loyal to her husband throughout the scandal. Washington, his great friend and ally, also stuck by Alexander during the whole ordeal.

Through all of this, Alexander was back at his old job, working as a lawyer. He took cases he believed in for free, but turned down big cases if he didn't agree with them—even when it meant he'd lose a large fee.

Alexander was also making plans to build his family a home. Up until then, they had rented homes in the city or lived in a summer place in the countryside. In upper Manhattan, in what is now a part of Harlem called Hamilton Heights, Alexander built a large house on a plot of open land. He named the house after his father's old estate back in Scotland—the Grange.

Napoleon Bonaparte

In 1798, the young man who "wanted a war" got one more shot. In France, Napoleon Bonaparte was greatly expanding his power and some worried that the fighting in Europe would spill across the Atlantic to

The former home of the Hamilton family, the Grange, is now a National Memorial located in New York City.

Visitors today can go inside the Grange to explore where Alexander and his family lived.

involve America. The president at the time, John Adams, called on Washington to lead the army again. Washington, of course, insisted on having Alexander as his second in command. Adams hated Alexander, but Adams gave in to the former president. Adams put Alexander in charge of the army, under Washington.

Later that year, on December 14, Washington passed away. With Washington's death, Alexander lost not only a great friend, but also a powerful and influential protector. Of his friend's passing, Alexander wrote, "The very painful event...filled my heart with bitterness."

"I have been much indebted to the kindness of the General..."

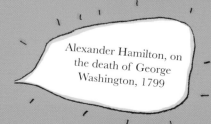

Alexander Hamilton, on the death of George Washington, 1799

83

Chapter 10

Alexander and his enemies

Alexander's strong opinions and actions made some people angry. Now, with Washington gone, his enemies could go after him.

John Adams

One person who really disliked Alexander was President John Adams. He believed that Alexander was helping the British. In addition, he felt that Alexander was proud, conceited, and lacking in principles. Once again, Alexander used his pen and paper to fight back. He wrote a pamphlet, or paper, filled with anti-Adams words. In it, he accused Adams of being insane and obsessed with himself.

What are principles?

A set of beliefs that guide how a person acts and speaks. Alexander's strong principles helped him do the right thing.

Alexander had gone too far with this pamphlet. Some Federalists were shocked and hurt. After all, Adams was a member of Alexander's political party. Because of this mean-spirited pamphlet, Alexander, the former Treasury Secretary, had lost the respect of some in his own party.

Despite this, Alexander persisted and spoke out against Adams during the presidential election of 1800. Adams and the Federalists lost the election, and the Democratic Republicans won—but there was a problem. The winners, Aaron Burr and Thomas Jefferson, were tied for the presidency. There would have to be a vote to decide which man would be president and which would be vice president.

Alexander had a horrible decision to make—should he back Jefferson, who he hated as a politician? Or should he support Burr, who he felt would be an untrustworthy leader? (According to Alexander,

Burr thought that politics was "honorable, fun, and very profitable." In fact, when Alexander was Treasury Secretary, Burr was shocked that he was not simply taking as much money as he wanted from the government.)

Because the vote ended up being tied, with 73 electoral college votes each, the members of the House of Representatives had to vote on it. Alexander decided to do what he thought was the right thing—he backed Jefferson for president. He convinced some of his fellow Federalists in the House to vote against Burr. Jefferson won a close vote, and because of this, the tension between Burr and Alexander

WHAT IS THE ELECTORAL COLLEGE?

The electoral college was set up by the Founding Fathers as a way to choose the president. First, the people vote. Then, the winner from each state is given a number of votes from each state based on its population. Those votes, represented by "electors," meet and do the actual voting for president. What it ends up meaning is that a person can become president, even if he (or she) actually gets fewer votes overall.

got worse. Two years later, Burr ran for governor of New York. Alexander jumped in again to stop Burr. When Burr lost, he set out to ruin his political enemy.

As if seeing Jefferson become president was not bad enough, tragedy struck Alexander in the fall of 1801. A man named George Eacker had spoken out against Alexander, and Philip Hamilton, his eldest son, tried to defend his father. Following the argument, the two men chose to fight a duel with pistols in Weehawken, New Jersey. Before the duel, Alexander suggested that Philip not try to kill Eacker, but rather aim elsewhere. He thought Eacker would do the same. Eacker didn't and Philip was shot. He died soon after, with his mother and father at his bedside. At the funeral, Alexander collapsed.

THE NEW YORK (EVENING) POST

Alexander's love of writing—and his interest in telling people what he thought—led him to start his own newspaper. He got money from investors and started the *New York Evening Post* in November 1801. The paper is still published today (though without the "Evening" part). In the paper's eighth issue, it printed the news of Philip Hamilton's death.

You might think after losing his son, Philip, that Alexander would stay away from duels. Unfortunately, that didn't happen. In 1804, Alexander said some unpleasant things about Burr at a dinner party. Another person who was there wrote a letter to a friend about it. The letter writer was actually happy that Alexander had spoken out so clearly against Burr. In one of those twists that history loves, the letter was apparently stolen. It was then printed in the newspapers. Burr saw it and was outraged—again. He challenged Alexander to a duel to resolve the dispute.

"My religious and moral principles are strongly opposed to the practice of dueling ... But it was impossible for me to avoid it."

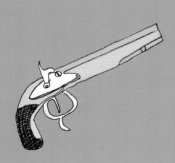

Alexander Hamilton, in a statement before his duel with Burr, 1804

It's hard for us today to understand why anyone would participate in a duel. How could two people shooting pistols at each other possibly end an argument or make up for an insult? The answer is, of course it can't. However, we have to understand that people thought differently back in Alexander's time. To most men, their

DUELING

Duels were used to settle disputes among wealthy or upper-class men until the mid-1800s. It was technically illegal, but it went on all the time in Europe and America. In a duel, two men fought with single-shot pistols or swords. Most duels ended with little damage, but some were deadly.

A pair of dueling pistols would often be stored in a wooden case.

honor was more important than their life. It was even more the case with Alexander, who always felt like he was an "outsider."

DID YOU KNOW?

Alexander was not new to duels. He was nearly involved in 12 of them during his lifetime!

Historians have looked at Alexander's past for signs as to why he could not simply ignore Burr or find another way out. They point again and again to the fact that he never really felt like a real "insider" in American politics and society. He felt that he constantly had to prove himself and his honor. In fact, Alexander had been challenged to other duels before his confrontation with Burr. Fortunately, no one was injured in any of them—but the outcome this time would be very different.

Chapter 11

The **duel** and the **end**

Alexander let his concern for his honor and reputation get in the way of his reason. A life that began with tragedy ended that way as well.

On the night before his duel with Aaron Burr, Alexander wrote a letter to his wife. It was to be opened if he did not survive the duel. In the letter, he tried to explain that he had to defend his honor. He said that he would not be able to live with himself if he did not. This way of thinking might not make much sense to us today, but that was how many people felt back then. He ended the letter with the sad words, "Adieu [goodbye] best of wives and best of Women. Embrace all my darling Children for me."

The two men rose early on July 11, 1804. They would cross

DID YOU KNOW?

Burr was not just an average politician at the time of his duel with Alexander. He was the vice president of the United States!

the Hudson River to duel in a field in Weehawken, New Jersey. Dueling was officially illegal, so they didn't want to be caught in New York City. The other side of the river was quiet and remote.

Each man had brought a "second," a sort of duel assistant. The men climbed into separate boats and were rowed across the Hudson. Alexander carried the pistol his son

had used. When the men reached the shore, they climbed to a bluff overlooking the river.

The seconds made sure the area was clear and then handed Burr and Alexander each a pistol. A doctor also came with them.

The men walked ten paces, or steps, away from each other. Then Alexander paused to put on his glasses. "I beg pardon for delaying you," he said to Burr.

Before the duel, Alexander told his second that, due to his Christian beliefs, he would not aim at Burr. Yet he would stand there, for his honor, while Burr shot at him. The seconds gave the signal to fire. Alexander shot at the sky. Burr shot Alexander in the side.

Dr. David Hosack was the doctor present at the duel.

Alexander's second rushed to his aid, as did a doctor who had come with them. Unfortunately, there was little they could do to help him. The round pistol ball had hit Alexander's liver. He was bleeding badly, but he was still conscious as they quickly carried him to the boat. Alexander was rowed back to New York City. His wife, Eliza, and some of his children were with him when he died the next day, on July 12, 1804.

During the duel between Alexander and Burr in 1804, Alexander aimed his pistol into the air to avoid hitting Burr. Burr, however, shot Alexander and fatally wounded him.

A huge funeral was held two days later. One historian said that pretty much everyone in New York City walked in the procession. Alexander's coffin was carried through the streets on a cart. His military hat and sword rested on top of the coffin.

The procession's final destination was Trinity Church (which still stands today), in lower Manhattan. After the mourners reached the church, the coffin was carried inside and the people packed the pews, or benches. Hundreds more stood outside the church, silently honoring Alexander.

Alexander's funeral at Trinity Church in New York City was packed with mourners.

Alexander's memorial and final resting place in Trinity Churchyard.

A longtime friend and fellow member of the Constitutional Convention, Gouverneur Morris, gave the eulogy, which is a talk given in honor of someone who has died. Morris had known Alexander for years. He spoke about Alexander's many contributions to the nation, about his

Gouverneur Morris

love of family, and about his courage. Then he asked everyone present to "protect his fame."

Alexander is buried in the Trinity Church Cemetery in what is today's Financial District of New York City. This is the center of America's banking industry, which his work made possible, in a country that might not exist without him.

"washington sought for splendid talents, for extensive information, and, above all, he sought for integrity—all these he found in **Hamilton**."

Gouverneur Morris,
in his eulogy for
Alexander, 1804

12

Alexander's legacy

In 2015, Alexander returned to the American stage in more ways than one. A theatrical performance reminded us of his importance.

Alexander died in a duel more than 200 years ago. In recent decades, Americans remembered him more for his place on the $10 bill than as the person responsible for the country's financial structure and a Founding Father. The historians knew about him, and his duel with Burr was always mentioned in stories about the Revolutionary War and its aftermath. In 2015, however, the public's interest in Alexander was about to change.

Alexander's face is on the United States' $10 bill.

Lin-Manuel Miranda

Today, Alexander is a household name because of a Broadway musical. On August 6, 2015, a massively creative man named Lin-Manuel Miranda released a new musical on Broadway. Using rap and hip-hop style songs and a completely different entertainment style, Miranda's *Hamilton: An American Musical* not only revolutionized Broadway, but it also changed how people thought of Alexander himself.

Miranda's belief was that this was a seriously important, interesting, and forward-thinking person who was not getting his due. Miranda focused on Alexander's immigrant status, his brave new way of

Hamilton: An American Musical is performed at the Richard Rodgers Theatre.

thinking of America, and his wisdom in setting up how America runs. Within days of the show's opening, its memorable songs were on millions of people's lips. Tickets sold out months in advance, it won 11 Tony Awards, and is now touring the world. *Hamilton: An American Musical* put Alexander and his work back in the spotlight.

BROADWAY AND THE TONY AWARDS

The heart of American theater is the Broadway district in New York City. Named for a wide avenue that runs through it, Broadway is home to more than 40 theaters that host plays, musicals, and other performances. People come from around the world to see the best in show business. Each year, top shows and actors on Broadway are honored with the Tony Awards.

DID YOU KNOW?

Today's American military forces include the United States' Army, Navy, Marines, and the Air Force.

Away from the stage, we can still feel Alexander's impact in quieter ways. His achievements made possible much of America's growth. He worked to give the federal government the authority to provide money for land and industry. By doing so, America's wealth grew.

The nation defended itself from foreign enemies using an army that Alexander knew would be vital to build. The economy boomed, thanks to a currency and a money system that he, as the first Treasury Secretary, invented. We have coins and paper money created by the mints he opened. Thousands of lives have been saved by the Coast Guard and the lighthouses that he helped build.

Today, many of the Revolutionary War heroes and Founding Fathers have been honored with monuments. Most of them are on the East Coast, in cities where those heroes lived, worked, and died to help create the United States. Alexander is no exception.

Along with the impressive marble block on his tomb, Alexander is remembered with monuments in his home town of New York City. For example, in Central Park a large granite statue of him was put up in 1880.

Memorial to Alexander Hamilton near the Great Lawn in Central Park.

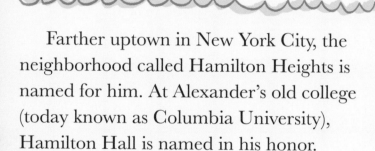

Farther uptown in New York City, the neighborhood called Hamilton Heights is named for him. At Alexander's old college (today known as Columbia University), Hamilton Hall is named in his honor.

In December 1960, the home that Alexander built for his family in upper Manhattan—the Grange—was declared a National Historic Landmark. The whole house was moved in its entirety (twice!), and has been restored to its former glory. Known today as Hamilton Grange, the estate is now run by the United States' National Park Service, and it is a popular tourist attraction.

Yet, although Alexander Hamilton was put on the $10 bill in 1928, no major monuments to him stand in Washington, D.C., as they do to George Washington and Thomas Jefferson.

Without Alexander, though, what would our national government be today? It's hard to say exactly, but what is undeniable is that the United States as it is today would be very different without the forward-thinking ideas he put into action. Historian Richard Payne said, "This, the United States, is Hamilton's monument." That's better than a building—not just for the brilliant kid from Nevis, but for all of us as well.

109

Alexander's
family tree

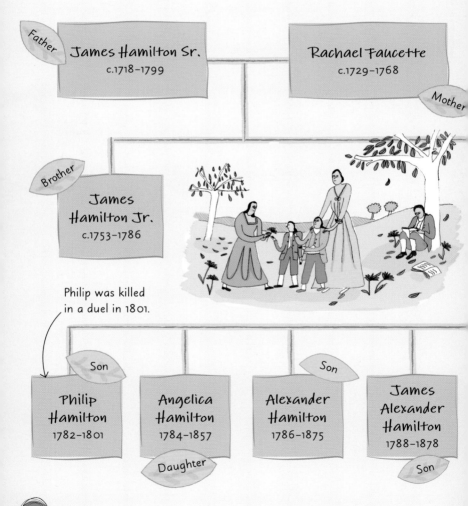

Father James Hamilton Sr.
c.1718–1799

Rachael Faucette
c.1729–1768 **Mother**

Brother James
Hamilton Jr.
c.1753–1786

Philip was killed
in a duel in 1801.

Son Philip
Hamilton
1782–1801

Angelica
Hamilton
1784–1857

Daughter

Alexander
Hamilton
1786–1875

Son James
Alexander
Hamilton
1788–1878

Son

Alexander married Eliza in 1780.

Alexander Hamilton

1757–1804

Wife

Elizabeth (Eliza) Schuyler

1757–1854

↳ She was the second daughter of General Philip Schuyler.

Son

John Church Hamilton

1792–1882

William Stephen Hamilton

1797–1850

Son

Daughter

Elizabeth Hamilton Holly

1799–1859

Son

Philip Hamilton

1802–1884

Timeline

Alexander's mother Rachael dies.

Alexander enters King's College (now called Columbia University) in New York City.

Alexander Hamilton is born on January 11 on Nevis, a Caribbean island.

| 1757 | 1766 | 1768 | 1772 | 1773 |

Alexander starts working as a clerk for Nicholas Cruger.

A hurricane hits the Caribbean. Later that year, Alexander moves to New York.

The Continental Congress passes the Declaration of Independence on July 4.

The Revolutionary War begins.

Alexander marries Elizabeth (Eliza) Schuyler at her family's mansion in Albany, New York.

1775 **1776** **1777** **1780** **1781**

Alexander becomes an aide-de-camp to George Washington.

Alexander leaves school and joins the Continental Army as a captain.

Alexander fights in the Battle of Yorktown.

The United States begins minting its own national coins.

Alexander becomes a lawyer.

George Washington becomes the first United States' president and appoints Alexander to be the first Secretary of the Treasury.

1782 1783 1787 1789 1792

The Revolutionary War ends.

Alexander is named a New York delegate to the Constitutional Convention, making him one of the Founding Fathers of the United States.

John Adams becomes president.

Burr challenges Alexander to a duel, and shoots him on July 11. Alexander dies on July 12.

1795   1797   1801   1804

Alexander returns to practicing law in New York, though he retains influence in the government.

Thomas Jefferson and Aaron Burr tie for the presidency in the electoral college, and Alexander helps Jefferson win.

Quiz

 Where was Alexander born?

 What did Alexander write about in a letter to his father that ended up getting published in the newspaper?

 What is the name of the revolutionary group that Alexander helped form before the war?

 What was the name of Alexander's wife?

 What did Alexander's New York Manumission Society fight against?

 What were Alexander's writings in support of the Constitution called?

 What state were Thomas Jefferson and James Madison from?

Do you remember what you've read?
How many of these questions about
Alexander's life can you answer?

 Alexander helped form the first United States Mint, which does what?

 Whose death in 1799 was Alexander very upset about?

 Who was Alexander's number one political enemy, who challenged him to a duel?

 Why did the duel take place in Weehawken, New Jersey, instead of New York City?

 What United States' currency is Alexander's face currently printed on?

Answers on page 128

Who's who?

Adams, John
(1735–1826) Founding Father and second president of the United States, from 1797 to 1801

Bonaparte, Napoleon
(1769–1821) French general and French emperor from 1804 to 1814/15

Burr, Aaron
(1756–1836) third vice president of the United States, from 1801 to 1805; Alexander's political enemy who killed him in a duel

Cruger, Nicholas
(1743–1800) New York merchant who employed Alexander on St. Croix

Eacker, George
(c.1774–1804) New York lawyer who killed Philip Hamilton in a duel

Faucette, Rachael
(c.1729–1768) Alexander's mother

Franklin, Benjamin
(1706–1790) Founding Father and printer, publisher, author, inventor, scientist, and diplomat

Hamilton, Elizabeth (Eliza) Schuyler
(1757–1854) Alexander's wife

Hamilton, James, Sr.
(c.1718–1799) Alexander's father

Hamilton, James, Jr.
(c.1753–1786) Alexander's brother

Hamilton, Philip
(1782–1801) Alexander's eldest son

Jefferson, Thomas
(1743–1826) draftsman of the Declaration of

Independence and third president of the United States, from 1801 to 1809

Laurens, John
(1754–1782) officer in the Revolutionary War who also served as an aide-de-camp to Washington

Madison, James
(1751–1836) Founding Father and fourth president of the United States, from 1809 to 1817

Miranda, Lin-Manuel
(1980–) American composer, playwright, and actor who wrote *Hamilton: An American Musical*

Mitchell, Ann Lytton Venton
(1743–1827) Alexander's first cousin who helped to pay for his education

Morris, Gouverneur
(1752–1816) American statesman and member of the Constitutional Convention; gave the eulogy at Alexander's funeral

Mulligan, Hercules
(1740–1825) an Irish-American member of the revolutionary group the Sons of Liberty

Reynolds, Maria
(1768–1828) the woman Alexander had an affair with

Schuyler, Philip
(1733–1804) American statesman and Alexander's father-in-law

Stevens, Edward
(c.1756–1834) Alexander's best friend as a child who became a physician and diplomat

Washington, George
(1732–1799) leader of the Continental Army, Founding Father, and first president of the United States, from 1789 to 1797

Glossary

aide-de-camp
military officer who assists another officer

Anti-Federalist
person who opposed the Constitution and was in favor of states' rights

assumption
to take on something, such as a debt, that is not yours

battalion
larger group made up of several smaller groups of soldiers in the army

bond
financial IOU—a certificate of a loan that is to be paid back at a specific later date

colony
any land or territory owned and controlled by another country

Congress
collective name for the two parts of the United States' legislature

Constitution
document listing the basic laws and rights of the United States and its citizens

Constitutional Convention
meeting in Philadelphia where the United States Constitution was written

Continental Army
army formed to fight Great Britain in the Revolutionary War

Continental Congress
gathering of delegates from each of the thirteen colonies, which became the governing body of the United States during the Revolutionary War

controversial
something that causes disagreement

Declaration of Independence
document that stated that the American colonies were no longer owned by Great Britain

delegate
representative; someone sent with power to act for others

duel
formal public fight used to settle a dispute between two people using weapons

electoral college
group of electors (representative voters) that chooses the United States president by casting votes based on who won the popular vote in their state

eloquent
well-spoken

endeavors
efforts

Federalist
person who wanted a strong national government and supported the Constitution

Federalist Papers
series of articles
written to influence
voters by answering
questions about how
the new Constitution
would work

Federal Reserve Bank
current central bank
of the United States

Founding Father
a member of the
Constitutional
Convention of 1787

general
high-ranking officer
who plans attacks
and leads troops

Hearts of Oak
voluntary militia
group formed in
pre-Revolutionary
War New York

Hessians
German soldiers hired
by the British to fight
for them during the
Revolutionary War

**House of
Representatives**
half of the United
States' legislature,
where the number
of representatives is
determined by the
population of each state

legislature
group of people who
make and change laws;
in the United States,
the legislature is made
up of the House of
Representatives and
the Senate

**New York
Manumission Society**
first antislavery
organization in
New York

originalists
people who review
documents, such as
the Constitution and the
Federalist Papers, to ensure
that laws are being
followed as the Founding
Fathers intended

principles
set of beliefs that guide how a person acts and speaks

ratification
act of giving legal approval to something

redoubt
building or area that gives protection to soldiers under attack

reinforcements
additional soldiers to strengthen an army

Revolutionary War
(1775–1783) war fought between Great Britain and thirteen of its colonies that declared independence as the United States of America; also called the American Revolution

Senate
half of the United States' legislature, where each state has two representatives

slavery
when a person is controlled and "owned" by another

Treasury
government department in charge of the country's finances

voracious
extremely eager about an activity

Index

Jj

Jefferson, Thomas 33, 55, 66, 67, 77, 85, 86, 106
judicial branch 57

Kk

King's College (New York) 25, 32

Ll

Laurens, John 62
Lavien, Peter 12
law 49, 51–52, 80
legacy 102–108
legislative branch 57, 65
Leutze, Emanuel 37, 38–39
Lexington, Battle of 28
lighthouses 74–75, 105
Long Island 35

Mm

Madison, James 57, 65, 66, 67, 77
Manhattan 35, 80, 107
marriage 44, 79
memorials 99, 106
mercenaries 36
military forces 105
Mints, United States 72–73, 105
Miranda, Lin-Manuel 103
money 72–73
monuments 106, 108

Morris, Gouverneur 100, 101
Mulligan, Hercules 25, 26, 30
musical 103–104

Nn

Nevis 8–11, 21, 27, 108
New Hampshire 63
New Jersey 35, 36–40
New World 8
New York City 24–27, 30, 34–35, 51, 54, 61, 66
New York Evening Post 88
New York Manumission Society 62

Oo

"originalists" 60
orphans 15

Pp

pamphlet, anti-Adams 84–85
paper money 73, 102, 105, 107
Payne, Richard 108
Philadelphia 66, 70–71, 72, 73
pistols, dueling 90
Princeton University 24, 40
principles 84

Acknowledgments

DK would like to thank: Rashika Kachroo for additional design help; Jolyon Goddard for additional editorial help; Jacqueline Hornberger for proofreading; Helen Peters for the index; Emily Kimball and Nishani Reed for legal advice; Nicole Scholet de Villavicencio for her expertise on Alexander's life; Stephanie Laird for literacy consulting; and Noah Harley for serving as our "Kid Editor."

The publisher would like to thank the following for their kind permission to reproduce their photographs:
(Key: a-above; b-below/bottom; c-center; f-far; l-left; r-right; t-top)
11 Alamy Stock Photo: robertharding. 13 Alamy Stock Photo: The Granger Collection. 17 Alamy Stock Photo: The Granger Collection. 19 Alamy Stock Photo: Andrew Duke (ca); World History Archive (c); INTERFOTO (cra); The Picture Art Collection (cr). 25 Getty Images: Rykoff Collection / CORBIS. 26 Alamy Stock Photo: Niday Picture Library. 28 Alamy Stock Photo: Archive Images. 31 Alamy Stock Photo: North Wind Picture Archives. 33 Library of Congress, Washington, D.C.: LC-USZ62-41929. 35 Library of Congress, Washington, D.C.: LC-USZC4-4970. 36 Alamy Stock Photo: Granger Historical Picture Archive. 38–39 Alamy Stock Photo: Rana Royalty free. 42 Library of Congress, Washington, D.C.: LC-DIG-pga-01368. 43 Alamy Stock Photo: Granger Historical Picture Archive. 47 Library of Congress, Washington, D.C.: LC-DIG-pga-01668. 53 Alamy Stock Photo: Everett Collection Historical. 58 Alamy Stock Photo: Mira. 59 Alamy Stock Photo: Ian Dagnall. 60 Alamy Stock Photo: Granger Historical Picture Archive. 65 Library of Congress, Washington, D.C.: LC-DIG-pga-10283. 66 Alamy Stock Photo: IanDagnall Computing. 67 Depositphotos Inc: tiger_barb. 68 Alamy Stock Photo: Steven Jones.

72 Alamy Stock Photo: Granger Historical Picture Archive. 73 Alamy Stock Photo: Brian Brown. 75 Alamy Stock Photo: Mira. 77 Library of Congress, Washington, D.C.: LC-USZ62-102555. 80 Alamy Stock Photo: Heritage Image Partnership Ltd. 81 Alamy Stock Photo: Hemis (t). Getty Images: Mike Coppola / Getty Images for National Park Service (b). 84 Getty Images: DEA / M. SEEMULLER / DeAgostini. 90 Alamy Stock Photo: Granger Historical Picture Archive. 95 Alamy Stock Photo: Old Paper Studios. 96–97 Alamy Stock Photo: The Granger Collection. 99 Alamy Stock Photo: Stuart Forster (b); Alfredo Maiquez / age fotostock (t). 100 Library of Congress, Washington, D.C.: LC-USZ62-45482. 102 Alamy Stock Photo: Ivan Vdovin. 103 Alamy Stock Photo: Ed Rooney (b). Getty Images: John Lamparski (t). 104 Getty Images: Fresh photos from all over the worls. 106 Alamy Stock Photo: simon leigh. 109 Getty Images: GraphicaArtis / Archive Photos. 111 Alamy Stock Photo: IanDagnall Computing

Cover images: *Front and Spine:* Getty Images: Kean Collection / Archive Photos

All other images © Dorling Kindersley
For further information see: www.dkimages.com

Page 108, quote source: Richard Payne, "PBS American Experience: Alexander Hamilton" (2007)

ANSWERS TO THE QUIZ ON PAGES 116–117

1. Nevis, an island in the Caribbean; 2. a hurricane that had hit the Caribbean; 3. Hearts of Oak; 4. Elizabeth (Eliza) Schuyler; 5. slavery; 6. the *Federalist Papers*; 7. Virginia; 8. it makes coins; 9. George Washington's; 10. Aaron Burr; 11. because dueling was illegal; 12. the $10 bill